Photo on cover: Author's father, Isaac Braun, standing back row directly behind his mother, in front of family house in Rodnitschnoje, Russia (1916)

MY ABANDONMENT,
THEIR TREASURE:

A MEMOIR ABOUT THE TRAVELLER GENE

John

Blessings!

Love

MY ABANDONMENT,
THEIR TREASURE:

A MEMOIR ABOUT THE TRAVELLER GENE

LORNE BRAUN

My Abandonment, Their Treasure:

A Memoir About The Traveller Gene

Table of Contents

Forward

Thanks to Omnia (Mona) Marzouk who gave me gentle permission to rekindle the spark for writing. Thanks to Joyce Rupp, 'the other Joyce', for encouraging my writing with walks, advice and lattes. Thanks to David McKenzie for taking a chance by sending me to live in Ethiopia and thereby facilitating my experience of a whole new world. Thanks to the many in Ethiopia who helped me to discover friendship and respect across borders. Thanks to my daughter Megan for forgiving my many absences on important dates in her formative years. Thanks to Joyce my wife and companion of 47+ years, whose love and understanding has sustained me. And finally, thanks to my parents but particularly to my father, the memory of whom has brought this book to life.

A caveat is that I write with intentions of integrity from both a distorting memory perspective and an imagining of what my father may have experienced. My apologies particularly to family members who may have other memories or imaginings.

Journey and Memory

I move when needed

When the pain of not moving

Is too much to bear

Isaac Jacob Braun was born in 1901 in Rodnitschnoje, a small Mennonite village in the southern Ural Mountain region of Russia, just north of what is now western Kazakhstan. His life was as ordinary as it could be, given his place as a middle child in an eleven sibling farm family existing within a communal framework with roots into 16th Century Europe. While the world marched towards a global war, militant activity within Russia fractured civilian peace. Mennonites, in addition to other groups, felt the sting of marauding militias and gangs. By the 1920s there were enough events for some to describe the Mennonite experience in Russia as a genocide. My grandparents sold their farm and possessions to buy passage for themselves and their 11 children out of Russia. This included my 23-year old father with his 18-year old wife and baby.

My father was a little-spoken man who said things without speaking. His grade 3 education belied a world of wisdom. His was a hard life which grew into success and comfort in his new world. I was a recipient of that comfort. And yet the reminders were there of a heritage rich in both commonly-held values and shared trauma. My father referred more to the values and less to the trauma that resulted in his family's flight from Russia to Canada in 1924. He never spoke of a desire to visit Russia. That was left to my sister, Virginia, and me to do in 2004. This brought a sense of completion and fulfillment, as if a piece of my story could now be written. This then is a story of our shared journeys.

I am traveller

E-zahk, was machst du in der zukunft?
Mutti, ich bin reisender. *

From birth, destined to be a traveller

Inate longings, lusting to wander

Sense of home

Gift of impermanence

What to take, what to leave

What shall my soul find?

Gathering tokens of innocence

For sustenance

Who are my companions?

Wonder, awe, naivete

Casting fear and inertia aside

Boldly proclaiming heart and home

Once more settled

For a time

Ever settled, ever restless

* Isaac, what do you want to be when you grow up? Mother,
I want to be a traveller

I am strong

Ich bin E-zahk!

Strength of the soil

Earth man furrow to toil

Sweat beating profit

Day beyond day giving thanks

Bounty birthed nurtured

Cradled safe provision for life

Blasphemers vile spewing pain

Trampling life's nurtured goodness

Holy taken wholly

Lost hope grief for solace unrequited

Patterns of fractured dream

Day beyond day fixation vexation

Huddled storming given to despair

Disingenuous futurist looking in space

Spaces unclaimed

Claimable unreachable

Selling soul and survival

Inner strength

Ich bin E-zahk!

I am strong

Silence approaches

I feel the silence approaching.

The violation.

Whether taken or not,

I feel loss.

The abandonment of shame.

Amoral wanderings.

Do I stare?

Where is the recrimination?

And the silence is gone

Replaced by unnamed reproach

Will they return?

Will I return?

I sit and wait

At the nexus of intention and invention

At the crossroads of reason and passion

At the joining of paralysis and flight

At the knife edge of clinging or falling

At the balance of owning or owing

At the moment of acceptance or rejection

It becomes clear to me that the decision

Is mine to make, to choose

To live with consequences

And then to sit and wait

For the next polarity

The shifting of tectonic plates

The shimmering beneath the glass

The expectation of change

From what is to what can be

I sit and wait

Travelling silence

Travelling silence

Open trajectory

Scraping pain

Dull remembering

Granting permission

Full soothing

Healing hurts

Raw scabs

Finding resolution

Kind hearing

Seeking comfort

Full closure

Memory

I remember

I do not remember

I want to remember

I want to forget

I try to remember

I remember and laugh

Side-splitting laugh til you cry

I remember and cry

Dull aching cry til you want to die

Laughing and crying again and again

Joy and contentment

Pain and resentment

The coin tosses and flips

Do I deserve either or neither

I remember it all

I remember nothing

I remember

well well

you know how you wake up and slowly focus and wonder
what the day will bring and look out to see sun or not and
smell the coffee real or imagined and wonder why yesterday
was the way it was and think that is most strange and then
you wonder if you are awake or not and think how deeply the
wounds hold you and you are never ever going back to that
way of thinking and being and then the sun does shine so
brightly that you are blinded but in your blindness you can
see and you hear that voice but cannot distinguish the words
but their warmth melts you and you can fly so no one can
hold you back and you soar through the clouds and fall to
earths verdant mattress and you sink to depths of an unknown
source but somehow feel at home and yet the pull of homes
known smells and sounds and colours cannot compete with
the comfort tentacles that enfold your soul and leave you
breathless while revealing a tiny sprig of hope that you
examine microscopically and find the suns reflection and
moons shadow and then remember why you happened to fly
and fall at the same time and you see that life is circular and
precious and unknowable and mysterious and challenging
and frightful and wondrous all at the same time and that life
is to be celebrated

It was the house

The house and the people

But the house held my attention

Its strength its sense of everlasting

The rootedness

The house of my people

The wall-writing strange to strangers

Strangers now living in my house

But why shouldn't strangers live in my house

It was now their house

My abandonment their treasure

I touch the walls

The walls that talk but don't

Their whispers my memory

Their whiteness and blackness my constraints

Wisps of smoke stoked stove

Stair wood worn filial pain and pleasure

Does the house remember?

Do the strangers know their legacy?

The mortar firm no gaps for secrets

The house knows all but only tells the knowing

I pull back and see through distance what

I could never see touch smell hear feel

My sense of grounding is this house

This house that knows and tells not

My people have moved but I will not shirk duty of

permanence

My frame yet lives

Rodnitschnoje

I step into imagined time

Your world my longing to know

Is this what it felt like?

Am I feeling your soul?

Earth-washed sorrow

Tears onto frames welded shut

Opening no more

Hearts asunder

Pleading for mercy

Yet too far removed

Is this what it felt like?

Stoic responses

Blinkers no wide view

Worlds in collision

Shattered dreams and bodies

Bloodied for naught

Is this what it felt like?

Did you ever believe it would end

Without your consent?

I touch the worn steps

To your room

Your 100-year old house

Still the strongest in the village

I see you in the bricks

Solid in repose

Your visage calls me from the portals

You whisper me home

Welcomed by unshaven chin

Wordless breath

I strain to hear the words

Your lament longing light

Your cradle and caress

Is this what it felt like?

Generations

I am, and I always was.

I live in my people

Generations upon generations

Thousands upon thousands *

I am life and death

Joy and suffering

Longing and lament

Lasting and ever

Hear my newborn cry

Before I am born I was prepared

I am and I belong

My people journey

Attach detach re-attach

Our life is our grounding

Cry with me for losses

Past present and future

But I am strong

I survive, I am

I will be

* From Chariots in the Smoke, Margaret Epp, Kindred Press, 1990

Would I?

Would I go back?

To carefree childhood days

With ominous clouds?

To family protection

With whispered warnings?

To macho teen bombast

With bullets flying?

To downcast heart

With fear rising?

Would I go back?

To play with abandon?

To love without limit?

To resist with conviction?

To accept without friction?

Would I go back?

Knowing that a child

Can remain pure?

Knowing that a family

Can sustain heartache?

Knowing that a man

Can retain dignity?

Knowing that a soul

Can entertain paradox?

Would I go back?

To encourage that child?

To comfort that family?

To motivate that boy?

To protect that soul?

Would I go back?

To laugh?

To cry?

To die?

To live?

Would I go back?

Sometimes

I sometimes go to a land of unknowing

Where my dreams and waking coexist

The taste of fear gives rise to terror

My heart shrivels inward

Beating drum like silent screams

Sweat streaming flowing to carry me away

Catatonic catharsis washing me clean

I awake to torment, my accusers mute

Gaunt visage sunken courage

Breathless I watch my past rotate

Around vindictiveness and passivity

I am alone

My thoughts are not my own

Illusions in frailty, futility

Knowing the unknowing

And when my courage rises

Daring to be seen

My shame overwhelmingly calming

My need for redemption

Was I to blame? We surround our

Need for answers with questions

That have no answers

That go to places where

Dreams and waking coexist

At the edge

I sit at the edge of the world and see

Infinite beauty with newfound eyes

I scour the hidden places

Beneath the clouds layered

Shreds of hope become real

Where do I find wisdom

But in the search

And in the searching find myself

Pieces of my soul flying

To the magnetic core

As if needing to be absolved

Of birthright abused

And yet there is grace

The humbling power lifting all

And kindness restores me

So my kindness can restore others

And the edge is now blurred

And my confusion takes me away

And I don't know where home is

Yet I sense comfort and knowingness

And I am at the edge of the world

And I see home calling

And it is sweet and pure

And my waking is asleep

Tracings of grace

The expectations are too great

I am defeated before I begin

Is this the road more traveled? Has it been in vain?

I started with the will to achieve. We are achievers

I was well cared for. My success was in my heritage

A layering of hopes upon which rested my confidence

How does legacy become corrupted?

Our arrogance our downfall

Had our migrations always been preceded by that fatal flaw?

What then of future migrations?

Through a mirror dimly I see the distortions of pain

Indiscernible motions, indistinguishable patterns

Am I now immobilized?

An impotent futurist wandering through time?

And yet I can see and taste and hear and touch

The tracings of grace that have carried us, have carried me,

Through anguished abandonment to sanctified recovery.

The wholeness we seek is the beauty you provide.

We are more than the sum of our flaws.

Like Kintsugi, our brokenness transmits your light

For the world to see

Land and Longing

I have held the land

Sifting dry through my fingers

And yet I see life

Like previous generations of Mennonites, my father understood farming. Even with other skills or trade qualifications, a Mennonite was a farmer. The land was part of his being. The departure from land necessitated an arrival to land; that was a given. What may have started as land work to feed the family became land acquisition and amassing to build security. For my father the 1920s to 1940s in Saskatchewan and then British Columbia were a means of using land to build security for his family. There was little knowledge, or at least acknowledgment, that land given to Mennonites upon their arrival in Canada was unceded First Nations territory. My introduction to this issue happened through the Canada Truth and Reconciliation Commission hearings in Vancouver in 2013. Fortunately the friends I have who have First Nations heritage graciously accept my tentative steps on a shared journey.

When my journeys have taken me away from home, I have met many people who similarly are attached to land. I recall the indentured tea plucker in Sri Lanka who longed for his own land even as he showed me his labourer's card indicated going deeper in debt to the land owner each month. I tremble at the memory of seeing thousands upon thousands of newly arrived Somalis in an Ethiopian Ogaden refugee camp, their vacant stares of loss shaming me in my comparative excess. I struggle to understand the seeming wilfulness of mass flooding in Mozambique caused by water mismanagement in Zambia, taking away the precious commodity of land for many. I recall the disproportionate impact of Hurricane Mitch in Honduras on the poor who are forced to live in erosion prone lands yet who welcomed me with dignity and grace.

In our common humanity, we find the means of attachment which fulfill our desires to provide for ourselves, our family, and our community. As land can ground us in each of these spheres, so also can it be the means of separation and division. We can lose sight of the difference between land as a means to security and land as an end in itself.

The fact, and mythology, of Mennonite land success has driven the narratives of farming success leading to persecution followed by migration.

What choice did I have?

Must I now follow my brothers?

I am still a child

Songs sung on mother's knee

Songs of our fathers

Ploughshares now to arms

What have i done?

Retribution tribulation

My god, have I forsaken you?

Father forgive also me

Choice redeemed

But will the land receive me again?

Blood to soil

Earth washed over and over

The lonely road

I am overcome by loss

My despair my torment

I cry to you in my abandonment

Must I travel the lonely road?

I accept my ill fortune

But do not relinquish hope

I bridge the chasm of discontent

With longing in my heart

My search for calm

A plea for peace

Still waters covering the rage

My soul faints black

The agony a reminder of past loss.

What has become of my people?

A dispersed band of emigres

Drifting through haunted re-awakenings.

Will we arrive survive thrive?

And what losses will follow us here?

Thin places

I have seen the thin place between

The shadows and the knowing

Scraped and escaped, but to what purpose?

A tension stretched to bare souls

That sense the urgency of time

The liminal space knife edge thin

Teetering on grace-filled toeholds

The abyss waiting to swallow

And yet the thin place comforts

Is this what has always been?

Is this what my people have endured?

I have lived the thin space between

The static and the flowing

Shorn and reborn, but to what purpose?

The scars the reminders of

Urges that do not quench

Habitual murmurings of time past

Where lines fade into wandering

And where have we come to?

And when will the wandering end?

I have dreamed the thin space between

The real and the imagined

Crying and defying, but to what purpose?

My losses are humbling uncountable

Pain deadens and yet I breathe

The joy of uncharted waters

The veil not yet lifted

And how will I know I have arrived?

And will disappointment win the day?

I am living the thin place between

The here and the promised

Stooping and recouping, but to what purpose?

Sin and salvation intertwined

In the dance of recovered hope

Twisted fate shaking all semblance of normal

While winter storms gather in

Preparation for fulfillment

Of thin places realized

Therefore do we give thanks?

And in doing so are we redeemed?

Our truth

Gasp for breath

I can't breathe

What is it that takes me back

Jackboots pounding

Breath muted

Isolation flash fear

Moments torn from teeth-bared reality

Snarling hounds flesh tearing

Run run gasping

I can't breathe

Do we hide? From whom?

Red and white scissoring

Taking pieces at will

Dashing our dreams our hopes

We are exposed hunted objects

A game of dire consequence

We become ghosts

Here but not

Spirits of a world to come

Where we will breathe again

But for now we run and run

Prayer for the oppressed

By the barren prairie we sat and wept

When we remembered the golden steppes.

There on the jack pines we hung our scythes,

For there our sponsors asked us for songs,

Our previously landed families demanded songs of joy,

They said, "Sing us one of the songs of the colony!"

How can we sing the songs of the Lord

While in a foreign land?

We are the exiled come from afar

Our souls ever moving

Displaced evermore

Can we even remember a time and a place of tranquility?

Will our scythes cut the binds that restrain?

May we never forget the joy that clings to us

Beyond torment and longing

May we never relinquish the joy that lives within

Our lives, our loves

Our fears, our tears.

What has sustained us, held us

In its grip, its permanence?

Our story

Told in pieces, forever

Held open to scrutiny for all

To see God's work and yet

Who will remind us of our travail?

Empty wanderings that bear witness

To blood shed for the sins of removal

From the pain of remaining steadfast in suffering.

And to those who will not remember

We find solace in the knowing for all has come to light

We who reap the whirlwind of justice

Seen in a prism of diaspora memory

Faint hope of recovering dignity.

Who has seen the earth shattered?

While flight is taken

And sight forsaken

While right is expected

And terror rejected.

We return to look once more

And see the invisible indivisible

One who sustains retains

Our gentleness lying on the altar

Sacrifice as it has always been

The movement of the people

Spirit-whispered

We hear and obey.

And still the sepia portraits belie deeper movement

Of longing, of rootedness

To the soil, the great provider

Our sustenance

The work of our hands

The toil to which we owe our lives.

We are grounded and resolute

Connected to the vein of life flowing deep below us

The land gives us energy

We repay the creator with our labour

We give thanks always.

Do we curse our tattered history?

The legacy of our wanderings?

We follow the dream weaver who casts a beckoning spell

Our journey is not over

We move as one flesh

Returning as we must to the wanderings of our forefathers

Who will guide us

To the land next promised.

We do not despair of our impermanence

Our souls are threaded in a filament of trust

And we will be carried

As always in the hands

Of our beloved.

Our home is before us

We measure the steps

That provide grace and absolution

For sins of self-reliance.

And we are home

Once again in the hands of the one

Who has fashioned us to transience

And calls us to herself

Even as we are blind

To the manna.

And we are safe

Even as we do not comprehend

The judgment that has come to us.

And we are known

Even as we fail to recognize

The patterns we have repeated.

And we are loved

Even as we beg to be allowed

To wander for a while longer.

And we are forgiven

Even as we forget

Who has carried us on the journey.

Land

Mother land Father land Child land

Birthing nourishing sustaining cradling

in life and death

Rich fertile in my veins sinews

I am land

Tears of toil sweat ambition promise

Our land

The land of our fathers mothers

sons daughters still born and stillborn

dust to dust

We are people of the land

Together ways our ways

Spoken and unspoken

Generation upon generation

Life blood always the land

Will we remain?

Will we thrive survive?

Moving to new land renewal and hope

New land to caress bring forth

Emboldened to justice

We are simple and simply landed

Our complexity the strands

that weave and root us

Our Saviour the land which

both binds and frees us

Our hope the promise of land everlasting

Settler confession

Struggle to know
Truth be known
Settler journeying
Eating all in its path

Truth unspoken
Truths unknown
Eaten by the all-knowing ones

Painful remembering
Insulating hive-homes
No crossing tracks
Pure manifest destiny

Truths unwanted
Truths restructured
Ignored by the all-powerful ones

Creator haunting
Truth be found
Journeys unending

What have I stolen from you, Christy?

Oh, it wasn't me, technically
It wasn't me... and yet

Absolution, restitution, double helix
Meeting when we hit rock bottom

Raven, coyote, trickster, creator,
God three in one, duality shape shifted

Where can I run to from?

Where is our meeting ground common?

Hope eternal resting shared space

What can I return to you, Christy?
My gift, my friendship, my admiration,
My pledge of trust

Oh, it wasn't me, technically
It wasn't me...and yet

The hope we see

Mouse bear Buffalo eagle

Playful giant foraging regal

Scurrying broken seldom spoken

Never token

Once proudly covering massed plains

What has become of you?

Perhaps the wrong question asked

My silence my shame

Where is my apology forgiveness?

My blindness unaware of what comes next

My pain unfiltered guilty as charged

Condemned to death row on row

Seeing not what might have been

But what still could be

From the ashes the flowers bloom

My soul is awake restored

South west north east

Let us feast

Return to Mother Earth rest

Lest we forget not

Our trespasses but those

Who remain

Our stain washed white black yellow red

The thread of hope we see

Come with me

Can you bear to hear my stories again?

The air was sweet with

The laughter of children

Running barefoot through rich loam

Barnyard friends clucking and cackling

Carefree and cared for

Hard times gathering but not yet ripe

We would fly the idle worlds

Of imagination and longing

Too young to be calloused

Too old to be naive

The sun would meet us each day and yet

The storms were never far away

We grouped ourselves in battalions to fight

The unknown imminent enemy

Who knew the unfolding stain of death

Would follow us like a stench of fog

That would remain in our nostrils forever

Robbing us of our childhood

Old enough for the callouses to bleed, and

Old enough for our naivety to be transformed

Into searing pain

The telling of which gives no comfort

Resigned to be retold to those who can hear

Bread

When mother would bake bread

The world would stop

I was transported to a joy transcending

All pain and care would cease

The steaming loaf would appear

To be savoured and caressed

Imagining the molasses and grainy flavours

The texture of substance

Melting into pleasure

The sacred waiting time was for preparing

Our hearts to be filled

This bread was truly life

And in those times when bread was

No longer bread but a tiny fragment

Of hardscrabble

I would remember and savour the love

Tasting the care of kneading

Sweat and molasses the sacred elements

Now withheld

Home

I am your home now

Your nest your rest

I welcome your quirks and wrinkles

Your flotsam and dross

The lading you cannot cast off

The overburden you cannot scrape

You are welcome in my tent of belonging

My warmth for comfort

My heartbeat for solace

My breath for contentment

My being for shelter

God rest

Lead, still voice

Beyond reason and knowing

Settled in time and space

Chaos tumult noise

Beyond silence and void

Emptied of bliss and grace

Shelter peace calm

Beyond reserve and shadow

Collected for rhythm and place

Hallow, bless'd pulse

Beyond temper and showing

Consecrated by love's embrace

Injustice and Hope

How much is loss worth?

Do I dare to dream of change?

Will I smile again?

My father's and my having a clear sense of home and belonging gave both of us the experience of grounding to take to other places. Outside of North America my father loved the history and architecture of Europe, the big game of Eastern Africa, and the relationships he formed with a Palestinian refugee family in the West Bank camp of Ramallah. Being born with the need to wander fit my chosen career in overseas humanitarian work. Seeing camps of displaced persons in eastern Ethiopia brought to mind my father's escape journey from Russia. Riding the railways of India where more people seem to be on the outside of the rail cars than inside gave me a glimpse of my father's search for work during the Great Depression. Visiting a Palestinian camp inside Beirut where most residents have been born yet do not have Lebanese status brings me anger and shame that we still have not found a way for all to live free and just lives. My visits to Liberia brought me face to face with the evil of child combat and make me very thankful that my father was not conscripted during his last years in Russia before escape. North Korea was another matter entirely - a Kafkaesque mind bending experience that left me wondering in retrospect how it could ever be described to someone who hadn't experienced it themselves. Sadly my father had already passed away and I couldn't ask him if his Russian childhood had any similar bizarreness.

The moment when

I have seen the moment of discovery

When what has never been imagined

Never been thought possible Is

The moment when

Constant numbing of parasite infested liquid

Becomes pure nectar

The moment when

Constant jarring of repetitive gathering

Becomes pure joy

The moment when

The thought of a treasured future

Becomes possible

Who can dare to dream this future?

I have seen them

The mother with slung babe sleeping

The boy with the coat hanger car

The young girl braids flying

The first sip of clean water

Indelible expressions of ecstasy

It is a sacred moment

A moment when the possible Is

Exile?

My view of exile is coloured by where I am

Today I stand looking at a refugee camp of 600,000 souls on

the Ethiopian side of the Somali border

Souls because they are. Dying?

Perhaps some, but souls nonetheless

Deserving of dignity, humanity, being named

Each one is connected to others

Do I see them as connected to me?

I come as a voyeur

Shamefully I cannot avert my gaze

Defiantly returning eye contact, those that can. And what of

the others?

Threads and rags, clothes and enclosures

Is this even legal?

And the only water is tanker-trucked in

Endlessly, day after thirsty day

And still I look closer

There is pride of birth right

There is economy

There is determination

We will never be destroyed

We will survive

You may look but you may not take what is rightfully ours

And I remember my people

When does being exiled stop?

Wounds become scars

Torment becomes nightmare

Losses become aches

Flight becomes history

And so today I weep for the thousands I see and for my

people

Not because I fear their and our future

But rather for the injustice

Indian rails

Vacant accusing piercing

Millions of eyes

Daring me to invade their space

Their home on rails

Chaiwallahs and more

Masses upon masses

No reprieve

I follow the millions transported

Daily commutes to mega cities

Of steel and slum

And then we wait

And I see the intricacies of life

The love and pain and

Ordinariness of living at the stations

On the sidings and platforms

Dignity of human kindness even there

Can I see it through the accusing eyes?

Riding the rails

Glistening silver taking me nowhere

Visions of better ways

Swaying stalks over desiccated scrabble

Accompanied ghost eyes

Methodical iron clack clacking to nowhere

Riding to a better place

Hungry mouths home bellies distending

Wails of hunger hope

Horizons day after day empty

Hoped for hopeless ending nowhere

Promised lands forever imagined

Green fields someday

Salvation found but still I'm nowhere

Burj el-Barajneh

Hope in the faces

No begging, come join us

See how we play?

Football filtered through

Wire jungle matted

Power to serve free

See how we run?

Not from those who

Imprison but to those

Who love us

See how we smile?

You have not defeated us

We will rise

We will sing

We will exist, always

Palestinian camp

Osama, with missing pieces

Car attracting stares

Victim stance proud

Gift of God gifting

Others with refusal

To die to leave

Home stakes driven

Carpets laid neath stolen wires

Treated with contempt

And offering hospitality

In return

Cups water cold offered to

Friends and enemies alike

How long must this continue?

The work of evil

I have felt the embodiment

Of evil, crawling

Over my flesh

Bandoliers well used

Why are the locals

Backing away eyes drawn down?

My blood pulsing with

The gangsta rap

The evil is oblivious

Its work is done

Ammunition loaded

Quiet falls with the night

Dusk returns to peace

A snapshot of hell on earth

The children resume

Their dusty games

Weary, forgotten again, but alive…for now

Bricklayer dreams

He was a young bricklayer

On the path to Liberian success

Then I heard his history

Rambo-enamored child

Enlisting to feel the thrill of war

Pup handler to bayonet practice

Wave after wave of child gun-handlers

Fed to the slaughter

Why?

Of course no logic

Your pain magnified in trauma

Discarded to be cared for

By your home community

How could they? The beneficiaries

Of attacks and child kidnapping themselves

And yet healing comes

But what does a bricklayer dream of in the night?

After the killing

I happened upon a former child soldier

And asked for his story

It was normal and not

And then I tried to make sense

Why would a boy choose

The nearness of death?

I wondered about the stages

From onlooker to participant

Was there a moment

When he doubted?

What things were pulling him

Towards the killing?

I had looked into his eyes

But had I seen his soul?

His hands were of carpentry

And shoulders slumped

But could his finger

Forever pull the trigger?

I can imagine that world weariness

Comes from the awareness

That the pain we inflict on others

Is a burden of pain we then carry

The story was told matter-of-factly

In the way a child describes play

Without emotional context

Or understanding of impact

And without remorse

Or a sense of guilt

The larger question then becomes

One of inclusion.

How can a former child soldier

Be rehabilitated?

What a strange concept - to restore

To health or normal life

Can a former child soldier

Hope to live a normal life?

Can memories be expunged?

Can atrocities be forgiven?

Can killings be undone?

Can life be resumed?

When I have prayed

I don't intend to minimize the strength we draw

From constant communion with Creator

But there are certain times

When special application seems to be warranted

Can a rock have the same impact as a gun?

In retrospect I wonder how my mind works

I feel unworthy

And realize that the grace that protects

Is the same as the grace that privileges

Me to feel empathy

I hover above myself not knowing if I am victim

Or perpetrator

Or both

Do I pray for courage or truth?

For resolution or restitution?

For absolution or forgetfulness?

And when I no longer see the ghosts

I retreat to my memories

Of pain and perception

Of slight and rejection

And to whom shall I now pray?

The Kims and I

Kim 123 is quite a handle

The father the son and the next one

Kim 123 has cornered the market

From ex-Red dawn to the unsettling son

Kim 123 is everywhere

They see they hear and they stifle

Kim 123 will plan your tour

From the minders to the rifle

Kim 123 from cradle to grave

The Juche will protect you

Kim 123 with power to save

From foreigners out to get you

Kim 123 has lost its daddy

The sugar no longer on site

Kim 123 will go it alone

The nukes are ready tonight

Kim 123 is more than a fable

No one could make this up

Kim 123 is setting the table

So kimchi we will sup

Kim 123 has got my vote

For weirdest leader on earth

Kim 123 triune deity

Small wonder we rue your birth

After dark

And then I met him

In a cafe in the capital

He was on a death list

We met in the dark

I wanted to understand

What it was like and

Whether it was worth it

It is for the children, he said

Those who live in fear

Those whose hope has been suppressed

How can I not give them some light

It was not lost on me that

His life was now in the shadows

Are you fearful?

That is not the right question

You should ask if it is right

And living or dying does not

Change that fact

But how do you continue?

That is not the right question

One foot follows the other

Muscle memory overcomes fatigue

How do you grieve?

It is true there are losses

But each one is a legacy

That reinforces our resolve

Will the evil win?

Our responsibility is to fight

In small ways, one by one

Each child a precious gift

What do you tell the children?

That darkness is not forever

That there is good if you look for it

That the heart can love endlessly

And then he left

In the dark

On a death list

In the circle

I sit in stillness in the circle

Sharing expectations

That we drink from a common cup

Of experiences

I do not know you

Barely knowing myself

Your words not of my understanding

And yet we bond in common intent

Your smile and tears

Need no interpretation

Your subsistence and my excess

Are subsumed in wanting

What is best for our children

We survive so they can thrive

Your toil and my spoil

Both speak to love

I hear my forebear longings

In your voiced desires

Did they at times feel hopeless?

Could they imagine my life now?

Is my being here in the circle

A witness to their faithfulness?

You challenge me

You demand change

And in the meeting of

Subsistence and excess

Our intent is transformed

Into another way

On the way

I hear the young girl's laugh

At the sound of pure water

Surging through mountain slope pipes

The sight of wonder

At the prospect of reliable clean water

And I ask why.

Why is this an effort?

Is this not her right?

We come into the world unaffected

And assuming our place, rightful and true

And we believe our lives are just

Until we realize they are not.

The claims of others surround and impede.

Decisions of our choosing are dim reflections

Of the realities of others

And we live and die

On the way to self-realization

I see myself in the injustice

The decisions of my choosing

Create systems of inequity

Whose tendrils cross the world

Bridging consumer and producer

Over divides of space and understanding.

And what am I to do

With knowledge of complicity?

I cannot save the world

I can acknowledgment the impact of my choices

I cannot protect my lifestyle

My future choices will determine how I live

I cannot absolve my society through my action

I can only do my part

I see the young child balancing

A water pail on her head

Mirroring her mother's path

I see the hardship of her role

And yet it is not mine to correct

I stand alongside and together

We marvel at the gift of abundant water

Clean and life-giving

Show me the world

I asked a man to show me the world

Let me learn

Teach me

I want to see and understand

Well first you need to know

Where to look

I can do that for you

Come here

Do you see that door?

That's where we'll start to find

What you're looking for

But how do you even know

What I'm looking for?

That's why I'm answering and you're asking

First you've got to look for clues

What do you mean, clues?

See that purple dog?

Now that just is not right

That's a clue

So I look for colours that

Don't match what they're on?

That's a good start

Let's take a break and review

What you've learned

Either I shouldn't follow dogs

Or anything purple

Or purple dogs

Excellent

Now where would you like to go?

Well I think I should get out of town

You know the world is bigger than my town

It is true that there is some greener grass

But also some browner and redder

And sometimes even purpler

So now you're telling me

Through that door may be

Things that don't make sense in my town?

That's exactly right

So is that a reason not to go?

Only you can say whether

You want to chance it

If I don't like it can I forget it ever happened?

Now that's the tricky part

Some of the questions you're asking

May not have answers

But what I can guarantee

Is that once you start

You won't be able to stop

Are you sure you want to see the world?

Yes, I whispered hesitantly

All right, take my hand

And the moment I did so

I was in a parched landscape

With thousands of tents

Babies crying

Emaciated bodies staring accusingly

What is this place I shuddered?

This is the place of obligation

It is rumoured to extend beyond our sight

But no one has been there

Come closer

You can see our fingerprints on their bodies

But why is that?

Because they are family

I'm sure you know some of them

And they even have very thin dogs here

But be careful, they can eat you

But where is the water?

Yes, that is a problem

You see those people at the well?

They wait day and night

For water that never comes

So why did you bring me here?

To solve the puzzle, of course

But there is much more to show you

See that doorway on the hillside?

And I took his hand

And we were in a plowed field

Deep brown soil ready for planting

Men walking behind oxen

Women preparing to plant seedlings

It looked like backbreaking work

But it felt honest and good

The dogs were still thin but smiling

Can I help?

I want to do my part

But you are not a farmer

And anyways that is not why you are here

I think I am learning that labour has value

That is true

But how does the field and the desert relate?

The only thing I see is that

The desert has no soil

Come, there is more to see

And instantly we were on a road

Walking with soldiers marching

They were a ragtag crew

Some limping, some almost barefoot

I did not know if they were coming from

Or going to battle

Do you want to ask them anything?

May I? Although I meant dare I?

I picked a boy of 16 and asked

Are you a soldier?

Yes sir, he said proudly.

Are you winning? I asked

That is a very strange question, he said

All I do is walk this way and that

Shoot my gun, and hope I don't die

But don't you want to do something else?

Be someone else?

Yes sir, he said, I want to see the world.

I have never been out of my village.

I shook my head in wonder

Why did you bring me here?

I can't even see any dogs

They were the first casualty

And childhood the second

This all seems a bit hopeless to me

Is there no joy here?

That's where you come in

Think of all the joyful things in your life

Don't you think these people have

Some joy they could share with you?

But we don't think that way in our town

And isn't that why you

Wanted me to show you the world?

Come, sit over here

Let's review what you've learned

People keep doing things until they can't

It is good to look around you

There are not enough dogs of all colours

I need to get more skills

And what about time?

Will I have enough?

That depends on you

If you use all you have you might get more

And what about worlds?

Are there more out there?

Look around and you will see

There are doors everywhere

And teachers everywhere

And dogs everywhere

And remember, your town will always be there

When you want to go home

Sonship and Love

There is a moment

When you think back on your life

That it all makes sense

I count myself fortunate in having the father I did. A reserved person by nature, he found it hard to show emotion let alone tell me he loved me. And yet I never doubted that he did. My parents had a strong love for each other. My father's strong need to travel was matched by my mother's strong need not to travel. However she encouraged him to do what he needed to do. He variously travelled individually with his five children. I believe he did so as a means of conferring blessing. I remember an evening sitting with my wife and my father on an escarpment in Tsavo East in Kenya overlooking zebra and elephants at a waterhole and hearing his regret at not having done more for us children. Forty years later I can say that he did well.

Whereas my mother's love was always clear and unconditional, I've needed to follow my father's wandering path to fully understand his relationship with me.

It occurs to me now, although I've apologized to my daughter for missing so many of her important life's events due to my own travels for work, I take pride that I have also passed on the traveller gene to her. With the best of intention I desire that she understands me in a similar way that I am now understanding my relationship with my father.

Warrior

You are the firstborn

The lineage and the legacy

You arrive in purity

And are bathed in splendour

You will be nurtured

As a treasure

You will be strong

And your word firm

And the day will come

When my blessing is given

For all to see

Your rightful place

And the gifts you were given

Are the gift you have become

We are a chosen people

Led by skill and calm

Your voice is reason spoken

With respect and consequence

The yoke is heavy

But the burden is light

As my strength fades

Your hand is secure

My frailty is before me

But your presence gives comfort

And in this condition

My soul is uneasy

Have I asked too much of you?

Has the cost been too steep?

I see the warrior in you

But I now recognize its shadow

The wisdom of strength

Is in its careful use

The balance to passion

Is found in compassion

The carrying out of our role

Cannot be at the expense of our soul

And now in my fading breath

I see you the warrior anew

Your hardness is a shield

Your softness is a comfort

Your coldness is resolve

Your warmth is inclusion

I see you and am at peace

The path of sonship

Flesh of my flesh

Bone of my bone

You are from and within me, son

I have given you my

Phobias and psychoses

You will find your way

As millions have done before you

Blame not for access is given you

For inestimable resources

To overcome all

Your path is yours alone

No-one has gone that path before

And no-one will follow

My peace and my pain I give you

Curse me not for I have

Loved you and will always

Love you

You are my beloved and I am pleased

Shawkat

You are my son in exile

A gift to me

A claim of mercy

My wanderings finding chance

Happenstance, that understanding

Of relationship, not

Blood, yet identity connected

My transitory your stationary

Your escape my satisfaction

Now sons, blood and not

Common channels of compassion

Rooted in faiths, belonging

Crafted for justice

And so much remaining undone

My blessings endure

Dad

Why do I find it hard to say I love you?

I lived your love for me even when you could not say it

I always knew it was there

A father's role is defined before accepted

You taught me your craft and skills

And modelled your worldview

Infused I was with you-ness

I was always proud of you

I always will be

An octogenarian and a septuagenarian walk into a bar...

What have I learned in my seventy years?

A handshake is stronger than a signature.

My father's word was his bond

Forged by intention and will

He was tough but fair

I heard the stories and felt the respect

But also sensed the shadow side

Location, location, location.

Place was a key component to success

Whether driven by opportunity or fate

The determination seemed to be

Like a rolling of loaded dice

With the result a foregone conclusion

Charity is not optional.

I suppose a self-made person doesn't

Need to be kind

The misshapen mold we inhabit can have

Sharps and crevices to hide both

Flaws and gold

Crying is not weakness.

We are fearfully and wonderfully made

With the wrapping and trapping of convention

The sum of our tears

Neither depletes nor exhausts our humanity

But rather sustains us

Forgiveness is a pearl of great price.

I heard the words only seldom

But they stay with me forever

It is not for me to say whether

The words cover a multitude of sins

But I want to believe they do

Family comes before everything.

Our enmeshed legacy can bind us

As a chafing irritant

Or a protecting cocoon

Notwithstanding closeted skeletons

We are who we are

Love shows itself in many ways.

My father was not demonstrative

Emotions were a feminine construct

He showed his love in tangible ways

I felt non-verbally lavished

For me it was enough

The glass is always half full.

I'm sure he had his doubts and worries

But I never knew his pessimism

He was driven to succeed

Loss might have been on his path but

He clearly saw the goal ahead

Faith was to be lived rather than spoken.

Not that he didn't believe in verbalizing

Rather it was an inner conviction

Cloaked in Anabaptist conventionality

Our history spoke volumes

And our lives were added to that history

Silence is golden.

Why say two words when one would do

It did however take years for me

To realize that one is definitely better

Than none

What more can you say?

Memory is a wonderful thing.

How do you sum up a life?

Despite saying one should not live with regret

I will say it now

I regret not saying this enough

I love you

Surviving

I look over at you and see a survivor.

You slayed the dragon!

But survival is so much more, isn't it.

The knowledge of beating a statistic

Means that someone else didn't.

Efforts of many for salvation of the few

The select

Was survival pre-ordained?

And I wonder what I have survived

Inertia? Guilt? An active imagination?

Who cares for the carer?

We survive entry into the world,

We arrive kicking and screaming,

Totally dependent on others.

We survive our upbringing

And find our way among peers

Sometimes bullied and scorned

Sometimes loved and celebrated

And we eventually question our existence.

Why me? How did I survive?

Survival is not an existential game show

With movement of pawns and kings

As if in a storm of choice and decision.

We walk through doors only to encounter

More doorways.

Survival can be overwhelming.

And I look at your strength and am amazed.

Reconciling the truth

We celebrate and we mourn

Progress and regress

But from whose perspective?

Can I really walk

In someone else's shoe? moccasin?

I am told there is truth

Verifiable

Quantifiable

Burned in blood truth

Soaked in tears truth

Mine trumps yours truth

Take it or leave it truth

Beckoning reckoning truth

Is there a moment of?

Does truth exist if we are not in it?

Existentially true but still we question why

We have the debate

And look for solutions that seem out of grasp

When we only need to look inside our souls

Make peace peacemakers be

Tribute

I stand with the swaying guardians filtering memories

You have returned to the land, ever grateful,

Ever hopeful that it was not in vain

The struggle both painful and affirming

You have given thanks

Your story is ended, and yet

I will it forward

Your departure, your legacy is

My story now

I listen to the wind, your whispers

My feet touching your grounding

The earth our common vessel

Yours to hold, mine to fill

My tears water your memories

Your comfort enfolds and holds me

And I walk into my striving with your grace

By your side

I go to the place your body lies

Neath grasses shorn of fault

We commune in silent comfort

Knowing all was said in time

Why then do I feel this open wound

That aches for your soothing?

Generations pass and our

Souls give birth to another

Holding fast the legacy of

Faith and wonder

Hand in hand through the ages

We wander til our body rests

Birthing what is to come

The gift of newness our reward

And I hear you whisper well done

Connected for life

You announced to the world you had arrived.

I had no doubt you were beautiful

and would change the world.

You had already changed mine.

I had no idea - one step ahead of the other;

and then you followed.

I was always proud of you,

but I know I could have said it more.

How many special events did I miss in your life?

Was the cost of my absence worth the benefit of what I was

doing?

I have always considered that my work called me

rather than I having chosen my calling.

But there is the rub - how does a calling co-exist with family?

Both have elements of being and doing.

Whenever I met with families in various countries, I would

think of you.

Are you safe? Are you secure? Are you happy?

I know I could have contacted you more when I was away.

My only consolation is that you grew more independent

through my absences.

And now my role is again shifting,

as a new generation arrives.

A new identity, grandfather, is added to the others.

I expand and adjust.

I am learning how to be and do in a new way.

Who I am has not changed

but I have an opportunity to learn how to set new priorities.

And then

At the end of the day, this day,

We give thanks

For the signs of wonder and hope

We give thanks

For the paths of struggle and loss

We are saddened

By our lack of faith and resolve

We are saddened

By our inability to reform and renew

And yet

At the end of the day, this day,

We look forward

To the night's rest

We look forward

To an awakening of spirit

We anticipate a dawning of light

But for now

At the end of the day, this day,

We are still,

And at peace

Lorne Braun lives in Richmond, BC, Canada with his wife Joyce. He writes poetry using the Notes app on his iPhone in the middle of the night or over latte at the Sanctuary Cafe. When not writing, he volunteers for the Rivendell Retreat Centre on Bowen Island, BC. Lorne is also on the International Panel of Elders of Initiatives of Change International and a mentor. He is currently also working on memoirs from his 35 years of involvement with humanitarian activity in low income countries.

Manufactured by Amazon.ca
Bolton, ON